1774

FELICITY'S
COOK
BOOK

D1567150

DISCARD

*A Peek at
Dining in the
Past with Meals
You Can Cook Today*

PLEASANT COMPANY PUBLICATIONS

Published by Pleasant Company Publications
For information, address: Book Editor, Pleasant Company Publications,
8400 Fairway Place, P.O. Box 620998, Middleton, WI 53562.

First Edition.
Printed in the United States of America.
98 99 WCR 10 9 8

PICTURE CREDITS
The following individuals and organizations have generously
given permission to reprint illustrations in this book:
Page 1—State Historical Society of Wisconsin; 2—Courtesy of the Mount
Vernon Ladies' Association (top); Taken from *Home Life in Colonial Days* by
Alice Morse Earle © 1954, The Macmillan Company (bottom); 3—Louisa Courtauld
(English, 1729-1807), George III Salver, ca. 1777, $7/8$ x 6 $3/8$ x 6 $3/8$ in., The National
Museum of Women in the Arts, silver collection assembled by Nancy Valentine,
purchased with funds donated by Mr. and Mrs. Oliver Grace and family (top);
Courtesy, Winterthur Museum (bottom); 5, 7, 9, 15, 23, 43—Colonial Williamsburg
Foundation; 6—Taken from *Colonial Kitchens, Their Furnishings, and Their Gardens*
by Frances Phipps © 1972, Hawthorn Books, Inc.; 11—Library of Congress;
18, 19—Courtesy, Winterthur Museum; 21, 33—Reproduced from *Back of the Big
House: The Architecture of Plantation Slavery*, by John Michael Vlach. Copyright
© 1993 by The University of North Carolina Press; 27—The Bettmann Archive;
31—Taken from *Antiques of American Childhood* by Katharine Morrison McClinton,
© 1970, Bramhall House; 35—Talbot County Historical Society; 39—Courtesy,
Winterthur Museum (detail, bottom); 41—Courtesy of Trustees, Victoria & Albert
Museum; 44—Reprinted by permission of the Putnam Publishing Group from *Field
Book of American Wild Flowers* by Ferdinand Schuyler Mathews. Copyright © 1955 by
Genevieve M. Hubbard and Norman Taylor. Renewed © 1983 by Norman Taylor.

Edited by Jodi Evert
Written by Polly Athan,
Rebecca Sample Bernstein, Terri Braun, and Jodi Evert
Designed and Art Directed by Jane S. Varda
Produced by Karen Bennett, Laura Paulini, and Pat Tuchscherer
Cover Illustration by Dan Andreasen
Inside Illustrations by Susan Mahal
Photography by Mark Salisbury
Historical and Picture Research by Polly Athan,
Rebecca Sample Bernstein, Terri Braun,
Jodi Evert, and Doreen Smith
Recipe Testing Coordinated by Jean doPico
Food Styling by Janice Bell
Prop Research by Leslie Cakora

Special thanks to The Colonial Williamsburg Foundation for providing
the glassware, crystal, fine china, teapot set, and silverware shown in the
photographs on pages 18, 24, 28, 29, 36, and 41. To order a free catalogue,
write to The Colonial Williamsburg Foundation, P.O. Box C.H.,
Williamsburg, VA 23187-1776, or call 1-800-446-9240.

Library of Congress Cataloging-in-Publication Data

Felicity's cookbook : a peek at dining in the past with meals you can
cook today. — 1st ed.
p. cm.
ISBN 1-56247-120-1 (softcover)
1. Cookery—Juvenile literature. 2. Cookery, American—Juvenile literature. 3. United
States—Social life and customs—Colonial period, ca. 1600-1775—Juvenile literature.
[1. Cookery, American. 2. United States—Social life and customs—Colonial period,
ca. 1600-1775.]
TX652.5.F454   1994   641.5—dc20   94-19194   CIP   AC

Contents

Special thanks to all the children and adults who tested the recipes and gave us their valuable comments:

Andrew Boersma and his mother Sharon Mason-Boersma
Shannon Boyce and her mother Leah Boyce
Anna Carlson and her mother Elizabeth Carlson
Michelle Endres and her mother Brenda Endres
Whitney Fahey and her mother Gail Fahey
Alex Frey and his mother Mary Ellen Frey
Larissa Frymark and her mother Mary Frymark
Carla Gilbertson and her mother Lois Gilbertson
Stephanie Hasz and her mother Lillian Hasz
Erin Kelly and her mother Sally Kelly
Melissa Lindsay and her mother Patty Lindsay
Meagan Lowenberg and her mother Cheryl Lowenberg
Alicia and Madeline Lux and their mother Stephanie Stender
Marianna March and her mother Donna March
Saree Olkes and her mother Judy Olkes
Kati Peiss and her mother Kristi Peiss
Courtney Ryan and her mother Debra Ryan
Nick Young and his mother Lois Young

8. Make sure your mixing bowls, pots, and pans are the right size. If they are too small, you'll probably spill. If pots and pans are too large, foods will burn more easily.

9. Clean up spills right away.

10. Pots and pans will be less likely to spill on the stove if you turn the handles toward the side.

11. Have an adult handle hot pans. Don't use the stove burners or the oven without permission or supervision.

12. Turn off the burner or the oven as soon as a dish is cooked.

13. Potholders and oven mitts will protect you from burns. Use them when you touch anything hot. Protect kitchen counters by putting trivets or cooling racks under hot pots and pans.

14. Keep hot foods hot and cold foods cold. If you plan to make things early and serve them later, store them properly. Foods that could spoil belong in the refrigerator. Wrap foods well.

15. If you decide to make a whole meal, be sure to plan so that all the food will be ready when you are ready to serve it.

16. Cleanup is part of cooking, too. Leave the kitchen at least as clean as you found it. Wash all the dishes, pots, and pans. Sweep the floor. Throw away the garbage.

COLONIAL MEASUREMENTS

There were no standard measuring cups and spoons in Felicity's time. Instead, recipes called for ingredients by weight. A good set of scales and weights was one of the most important pieces of kitchen equipment a colonial cook could have.

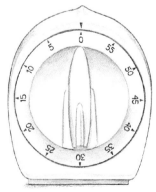

TIMING

When a recipe gives two cooking times—for example, when it says, "bake 25 to 30 minutes"—first set the timer for the shorter time. If the food is not done when the timer rings, give it more time.

BREAKFAST

*A **Dutch oven**, or bake kettle.*

Colonial breakfasts were served between eight and nine o'clock in the morning. In wealthy families, girls and women like Felicity and her mother did not usually prepare breakfast. Instead, slaves like Rose got up as early as 5:30 A.M. to rekindle the fire, get water, and begin cooking breakfast for the family.

Rose began by baking the breakfast bread. She heated the *Dutch oven*, or bake kettle, in the fireplace. It had short legs to keep the bread above the hot coals. While the bread was baking, Rose heated the griddle to make johnnycakes and breakfast puffs. Then she fixed meat left over from dinner the day before.

Rose made dressed eggs by broiling them. First, she heated a *salamander,* or long-handled shovel, in the fire until it was red-hot. Then she cracked the eggs into a frying pan and cooked them over the fire. When the eggs were set but not hard, she held the salamander over the eggs to cook the tops. There was no easy way to broil foods in 1774—cooks didn't have ovens with broilers as you do today.

A kitchen like Felicity's.

When everything was ready, Rose brought the food from the kitchen to a *sideboard* in the dining room. A sideboard is a piece of furniture that is used for serving food. It also holds linens and china. Felicity sometimes helped Rose at the sideboard by taking the food from the kitchen bowls and platters and putting it onto fine china for the table.

Rose usually served apple butter at breakfast. Felicity was proud to bring it to the table because she helped make it. Making apple butter was hard work. Felicity stirred huge pots of hot apple mush until her arms ached, and she had to be very careful not to let her petticoats get too near the flames!

BREAKFAST

꒰꒱

Apple Butter

•

Johnnycakes

•

Breakfast Puffs

•

Fried Ham with Gravy

•

Dressed Eggs

APPLE BUTTER

Spread sweet apple butter on your favorite breakfast bread.

INGREDIENTS

3 cups sweet apple cider
2 pounds apples
(about 6 large apples)
1/4 cup honey
1/2 teaspoon cinnamon
1/4 teaspoon ground cloves
1/4 teaspoon allspice

EQUIPMENT

Measuring cups
  and spoons
Large cooking pot with lid
Paring knife
Cutting board
Wooden spoon
Potato masher
4 empty jam jars with lids,
  8 ounces each
Paper towels

DIRECTIONS   *2 pints*

1. Measure the cider into the cooking pot. Cook the cider over medium heat until it *boils*, or bubbles quickly. Let the cider boil for 15 minutes.

2. While the cider boils, have an adult help you cut each apple into 4 sections.

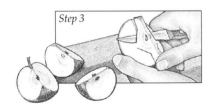

Step 3

3. Remove the core from each section and cut off the skin. Then cut the apple sections into smaller pieces.

4. Add the apples to the boiling cider.

5. Cover the cooking pot. Cook the apples over very low heat until they are tender, about 1 hour. Stir the apples often while they cook.

Step 6

6. Turn off the heat and remove the lid from the pot. Use the potato masher to mash the apples.

7. Stir in the honey, cinnamon, cloves, and allspice.

8. Turn the heat to low. Cook the apple mixture uncovered for about 30 minutes, or until it thickens. Stir often.

9. Turn off the heat and let the apple butter cool for 15 minutes in the pot.

10. While the apple butter cools, wash the jars in hot, soapy water. Then rinse them in hot water. Drain them on paper towels.

11. Have an adult spoon the apple butter into the jars. Serve apple butter on johnnycakes *(page 10)* or breakfast puffs *(page 12)*. Store the rest of the apple butter in the refrigerator or give some to friends. 🥄

KEEPING FOODS COOL

*Since colonists didn't have refrigerators, they kept foods like milk and butter cool in a **dependency,** or outbuilding, called a **dairy.** A dairy was sometimes built a foot or two below ground, usually over a cool spring. Thick walls under a big, overhanging roof kept the cool air inside. Vents let hot air escape.*

JOHNNYCAKES

Johnnycakes were also called "journey cakes" because they kept well on long trips.

INGREDIENTS

1 cup water
2 tablespoons butter
1 cup yellow cornmeal
$\frac{1}{2}$ teaspoon salt
$\frac{1}{2}$ teaspoon sugar
$\frac{1}{2}$ cup milk
Butter to grease skillet
Apple butter or your
    favorite syrup

EQUIPMENT

Measuring cups
    and spoons
Small saucepan
Medium mixing bowl
Potholder
Wooden spoon
Paper towels
12-inch skillet
Spatula
Ovenproof plate

DIRECTIONS   *12 cakes*

1. Heat the water and butter in the saucepan over medium-high heat until they *boil*, or bubble rapidly.

2. While the water and butter are boiling, put the cornmeal, salt, and sugar into the mixing bowl.

3. Have an adult pour the boiling water and butter into the mixing bowl. Add the milk and stir the batter until it is well mixed.

4. Use paper towels to grease the skillet with butter. Then heat the skillet over medium-low heat.

5. Drop 6 spoonfuls of batter into the skillet. Let the cakes cook about 5 minutes, until they are golden brown.

Step 5

Indian women scaring crows out of their cornfields.

CORN IN THE COLONIES

American Indians taught colonists how to grow corn. Fresh corn was eaten right off the cob or mixed into stews. But corn was usually dried and ground into cornmeal for bread. American Indians also made popcorn, which they sometimes served with maple syrup.

6. Use the spatula to turn over the cakes. Let the other side of each cake cook for another 5 minutes.

7. Use the spatula to move the cakes from the skillet to an ovenproof plate. Keep them warm in a 200° oven.

8. Drop a spoonful of butter into the hot skillet and let it melt. Tilt the pan to coat the bottom of the skillet evenly with the melted butter.

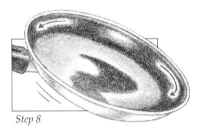

9. Cook the rest of the johnnycakes following steps 5 through 7.

10. When all the cakes are cooked, serve them with apple butter *(page 8)* or syrup. 🐌

11

BREAKFAST PUFFS

Serve these puffs while they're still warm from the oven.

INGREDIENTS

Shortening or butter
  to grease muffin pan
1 tablespoon butter
2 eggs
1 cup milk
1 cup flour
$\frac{1}{4}$ teaspoon salt
Apple butter, jam, or
  honey *(optional)*

EQUIPMENT

Paper towels
Muffin pan
Measuring cups
  and spoons
Small saucepan
Small mixing bowl
Fork
Mixing spoon
Medium mixing bowl
Potholders
Butter knife
Serving plate

DIRECTIONS   *6 puffs*

1. Preheat the oven to 425°.

2. Use paper towels to grease the muffin cups with shortening or butter. Put the muffin pan in the oven to heat.

3. Melt 1 tablespoon of butter in the small saucepan over low heat.

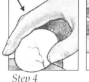
Step 4

4. While the butter melts, crack the eggs into the small mixing bowl. Use the fork to beat the eggs until they are light yellow.

5. Add the milk and melted butter to the eggs. Beat the liquid mixture with the fork until it is well mixed.

6. Stir the flour and salt together in the medium mixing bowl.

7. Slowly stir the liquid mixture into the flour mixture. Stir only until the mixture is blended. Do not overmix.

8. Have an adult remove the hot muffin pan from the oven.

9. Spoon batter into the muffin pan until each cup is ⅔ full.

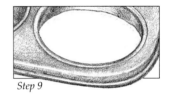
Step 9

10. Bake the breakfast puffs at 425° for 20 minutes. Then turn the heat down to 325° and bake the puffs for 15 minutes.

11. Have an adult remove the breakfast puffs from the oven.

12. Use a butter knife to loosen the sides of the breakfast puffs and remove them from the muffin cups.

Step 12

13. Arrange the breakfast puffs on a serving plate. Serve the puffs with apple butter *(page 8)*, jam, or honey while they are still warm. 🌿

FRIED HAM WITH GRAVY

In 1774, smoked hams were a specialty in Virginia, just as they are today.

INGREDIENTS

1 pound smoked ham slice
1/2 cup cold water
2 tablespoons fresh-
  brewed coffee

EQUIPMENT

Sharp knife
Cutting board
Large skillet
Fork
Serving plate
Tinfoil
Potholder
Metal container for grease
Measuring cup
  and spoon
Wooden spoon

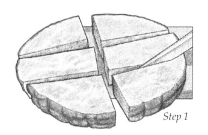

Step 1

Step 4

DIRECTIONS   *6 servings*

1. Cut the ham slice into serving-size pieces.

2. Warm the skillet over medium-low heat.

3. Add the ham pieces and fry them over low heat.

4. Use the fork to turn over the ham pieces several times to brown both sides evenly.

5. Then use the fork to move the fried ham pieces onto the serving plate.

6. Cover the plate with tinfoil to keep the ham warm.

7. If there is grease in the frying pan, have an adult pour it off into a metal container. Leave the drippings that are stuck to the bottom of the pan.

8. To make the gravy, pour the cold water and coffee over the drippings in the skillet.

9. Turn the heat to medium and stir the gravy mixture constantly.

10. When the gravy begins to *boil*, or bubble quickly, turn off the heat.

11. Remove the tinfoil from the serving plate.

12. Have an adult help you pour the gravy over the ham pieces and serve.

Hog

COLONIAL PIGS

In Felicity's time, pigs had long snouts, large tusks, and a ridge of bristles down their backs. Their owners often let them run wild! One man's pigs got into a crop of peanuts. The meat from these pigs was delicious, and soon peanut-fed ham was in high demand.

SMOKEHOUSES

*After butchering, meat was salted and then smoked in a **smokehouse** to help preserve it. Colonists used slow-burning fuel like corncobs for the fire. The meat took on the flavor of the fuel used. Families stored their meat in smokehouses until they needed it.*

DRESSED EGGS

These eggs are "dressed" with a dash of nutmeg.

INGREDIENTS

¼ cup butter
6 eggs
Salt
1 tablespoon water
Nutmeg

EQUIPMENT

Measuring cup
 and spoon
Skillet or dish with
 lid *(flameproof and ovenproof)*
Small cup
Potholders
Trivet
Spatula

DIRECTIONS   *6 servings*

1. Preheat the oven to broil.

2. Melt the butter in the skillet or dish over low heat. Don't let the butter burn.

3. Have an adult help you measure 1 tablespoon of melted butter into the small cup. Set the cup aside.

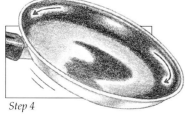

Step 4

Step 5

4. Tilt the cooking pan to spread the remaining melted butter evenly over the bottom of the pan.

5. Carefully crack the eggs into the skillet or dish. Try not to break the yolks.

6. Shake a little salt over the eggs. Then add the water.

7. Cover the pan and cook the eggs over low heat until the whites are set but not hard, about 5 minutes.

for dinner. She always made sure there was plenty of food in case unexpected guests stopped by.

An everyday dinner usually had two courses, with five dishes in each course. For large dinner parties, there might be as many as 21 dishes in each course! The first course might include meats, vegetables, soup, and bread. Veal, ham, chicken, and other meats might all be served at the same time! The second course included desserts like custard or whipped syllabub.

A middleboard.

Mrs. Merriman also taught Felicity how to arrange the table. In the English tradition, it was proper to set a balanced table. If there was a meat dish at one end of the table, there was a meat dish at the other end of the table to balance it. Pairs of matching bowls or platters were placed so that the table matched from side to side and corner to corner, too. After the meal, a hostess might serve more sweets. Dishes or pyramids of foods like dried fruits or candied flower petals might be arranged on a raised platform on the table called a *middleboard*.

DINNER

Chicken Pudding

•

Veal Balls

•

Sweet Potatoes and Apples

•

Sally Lunn Bread

•

Green Beans

•

Whipped Syllabub

19

CHICKEN PUDDING

In 1774, puddings were served both as main dishes and as desserts.

INGREDIENTS

2 tablespoons butter
2 pounds boneless,
    skinless chicken breasts
2 cups water
1 teaspoon salt
Shortening or butter to
    grease casserole dish
1½ cups flour
1 teaspoon salt
1½ teaspoons baking
    soda
3 tablespoons butter
3 eggs
1½ cups milk

EQUIPMENT

Measuring cups
    and spoons
Large skillet with lid
Tongs
Paper towels
2-quart casserole dish
Small mixing bowl
Wooden spoon
Small saucepan
Large mixing bowl
Potholders
Trivet
Serving spoon

DIRECTIONS   *6 servings*

1. Melt 2 tablespoons of butter in the skillet over medium heat.

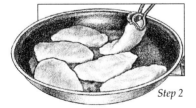
Step 2

2. Add the chicken breasts to the skillet. Turn the pieces with tongs until they are browned on both sides.

3. Measure the water and 1 teaspoon of salt into the skillet. When the water *boils*, or bubbles quickly, turn down the heat until the water *simmers*, or bubbles gently.

4. Cover the skillet and cook the chicken for ½ hour.

5. Use paper towels to grease the casserole dish with shortening or butter.

6. Use tongs to put the cooked chicken breasts into the casserole. Preheat the oven to 375°.

7. To make the batter for the chicken pudding, put the flour, salt, and baking soda in the small mixing bowl and stir them until they are well blended.

CHICKEN HOUSES

Colonists kept chickens in buildings called **chicken houses**. *The houses often had interesting details like the* **finial**, *or decorative knob, on the roof of the chicken house shown here.*

8. Melt 3 tablespoons of butter in the small saucepan over low heat.

9. Crack the eggs into the large mixing bowl and beat them together with the milk. Stir the melted butter into the eggs and milk.

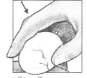

Step 9

10. Add the flour mixture to the liquid mixture. Beat this batter until it is smooth. Pour the batter over the chicken breasts in the casserole dish.

Step 10

11. Bake the chicken pudding for about 40 minutes, until the batter puffs up and turns golden brown.

12. Have an adult remove the chicken pudding from the oven and place it on a trivet at the table to serve. 🦅

VEAL BALLS

Hearty main dishes like veal balls were often served at colonial dinners.

INGREDIENTS

1 pound ground veal
A few sprigs of
   fresh parsley
1 tablespoon minced onion
$1/2$ teaspoon salt
$1/8$ teaspoon thyme
$1/8$ teaspoon pepper
$1/8$ teaspoon ground cloves
1 egg
2 tablespoons butter

EQUIPMENT

Large mixing bowl
Paring knife
Cutting board
Measuring spoons
Wooden spoon
Plate
Large skillet
Serving dish and spoon

DIRECTIONS   *24 veal balls*

1. Put the ground veal into the mixing bowl.

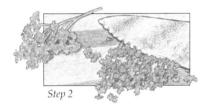

Step 2

2. Wash the parsley. Pull off several leaves and cut them into small pieces.

3. Add the parsley, minced onion, salt, thyme, pepper, and ground cloves to the veal.

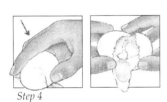

Step 4

4. Crack the egg into the mixing bowl.

5. Wash your hands. Mix all the ingredients together with your hands, or use the wooden spoon.

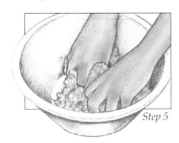

Step 5

6. Shape the meat mixture into 1-inch balls and put them on a plate. Wash your hands after handling the veal balls.

7. Melt the butter in the skillet over medium-low heat. Tilt the skillet to coat the bottom of the pan evenly with butter.

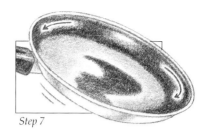
Step 7

8. Use the wooden spoon to move the veal balls from the plate to the skillet.

9. Cook the veal balls for 30 minutes. Stir them several times while they cook to brown the meat on all sides.

Step 9

10. Use the wooden spoon to move the cooked veal balls from the skillet to a serving dish. 🗶

DISH CROSSES

*In some wealthy households, the most important dish of each course was put in the middle of the table on a **dish cross**, a stand that raised that dish above the other dishes. The dish cross was made of two crossed bars on short legs. The bars could be shortened or extended to fit almost any size dish.*

SWEET POTATOES AND APPLES

To make this tasty dish, Felicity climbed to the roof of her house to pick apples!

INGREDIENTS

5 sweet potatoes
3 large apples
Shortening or butter to
    grease casserole dish
2 tablespoons butter
¾ cup maple syrup

EQUIPMENT

Fork
Cookie sheet
Potholders
Paring knife
Cutting board
Paper towels
Large casserole dish
    with lid
Measuring cup and spoon
Butter knife
Trivet

DIRECTIONS   *6 servings*

1. Preheat the oven to 350°.

2. Wash the sweet potatoes and pierce them several times with a fork. Put them on the cookie sheet and bake them on the center oven rack for about 1 hour, or until a fork pierces them easily.

3. Have an adult remove the potatoes from the oven and set them aside to cool.

4. Have an adult help you cut each apple into 4 sections. Remove the core from each section and cut off the skin. Then cut the apple sections into thin slices.

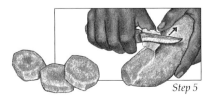
Step 4

5. Use the paring knife to pull the skins off the cooked sweet potatoes. Cut the potatoes into ½-inch slices.

Step 5

6. Use paper towels to grease the casserole dish with shortening or butter.

7. Use half of the sweet potato slices to cover the bottom of the casserole. Put half the apple slices on top of the potatoes.

8. Use the rest of the sweet potatoes to make the next layer. Then add the rest of the apples.

9. Cut the 2 tablespoons of butter into small pieces and place them on top of the apples. Pour the maple syrup over the top.

Step 9

10. Cover the casserole and bake the sweet potatoes and apples in the oven for 30 minutes.

11. Have an adult remove the casserole dish from the oven. Place the dish on a trivet at the table to serve. ❧

ROOT CELLARS

Root vegetables, like potatoes, sweet potatoes, turnips, and carrots, were stored in root cellars and covered with sand or dirt. Since root cellars were dug deep into the ground, they stayed cool and kept food from spoiling.

SALLY LUNN BREAD

Rose baked fresh bread for the Merriman family every morning.

INGREDIENTS

¾ cup milk
¼ cup warm water
1 package active dry yeast
6 tablespoons butter, softened
3 tablespoons sugar
2 eggs
3 cups flour
1¼ teaspoons salt
Shortening or butter to grease the pan

EQUIPMENT

Measuring cups and spoons
Small saucepan
Small bowl
Wooden spoon
Large mixing bowl
Medium mixing bowl
Clean kitchen towel
Paper towels
Tube pan or round 2-quart casserole dish
Potholders
Butter knife

DIRECTIONS   *1 loaf*

1. Measure the milk into the small saucepan and warm it over medium-low heat. Turn off the heat.

2. Measure the warm water into the small bowl. Add the yeast and stir. Then stir the warm milk into the yeast and water.

3. Measure the butter and sugar into the large mixing bowl. Stir them until they are creamy.

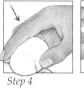

Step 4

4. Crack 1 egg into the large mixing bowl and beat the mixture. Add the second egg and beat the mixture again.

5. Stir the flour and salt together in the medium mixing bowl.

SUN-MOON BREAD

*Some people say Sally Lunn bread came from the French phrase for sun-moon, **soleil-lune** (so-lay-LOON). Each loaf has a golden top (sun) and white bottom (moon). In English, **soleil-lune** became "Sally Lunn," which is how the bread is known today.*

6. Stir about 1 cup of the flour mixture into the butter and sugar mixture. Then stir in about ⅓ of the yeast mixture.

7. Add more flour and beat the mixture. Then add more yeast and beat the mixture again. Continue adding yeast and flour in this way, beating the batter until it is smooth.

8. Cover the large mixing bowl with a clean towel and let the batter rise in a warm place for 1 hour. When the batter has doubled in size, remove the towel. Stir the batter quickly to take out the air.

Step 8

9. Use paper towels to grease the tube pan or round casserole dish with shortening or butter.

10. Pour the batter into the baking pan. Cover it with the towel. Let it rise for about 30 minutes, or until it has doubled again in size. Preheat the oven to 350° while the batter rises.

11. Remove the towel and bake the bread on the center oven rack for 40 to 45 minutes.

12. Have an adult take the bread out of the oven. Use the butter knife to loosen the bread from the sides of the pan. Turn the pan upside down to remove the bread.

Step 12

GREEN BEANS

*Green beans fresh from Felicity's garden
added color to the dinner table.*

INGREDIENTS

1 pound fresh green
  beans
$\frac{1}{2}$ cup cold water
$\frac{1}{2}$ teaspoon salt
1 tablespoon butter
Salt and pepper
$\frac{1}{4}$ cup heavy cream

EQUIPMENT

Colander
Measuring cups
  and spoons
2-quart saucepan with lid
Wooden spoon
Serving bowl and spoon

DIRECTIONS   *6 servings*

1. Put the beans into the colander and wash them at the sink.

2. Snap off both ends of the beans with your fingers.

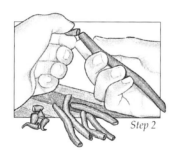
Step 2

3. Put the water and $\frac{1}{2}$ teaspoon salt into the saucepan. Heat the water over medium-high heat until it *boils*, or bubbles rapidly.

4. Put the beans into the water. Cover the saucepan and cook the beans for 5 minutes.

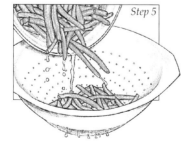
Step 5

5. Have an adult help you pour the beans and water into the colander. After the water has drained off, put the beans back into the saucepan.

6. Add the butter. Sprinkle on salt and pepper. Add the cream and stir gently to coat the beans well.

7. Spoon the beans into a bowl and serve.

WHIPPED SYLLABUB

INGREDIENTS

2 cups heavy
   whipping cream
2 lemons
1 orange
½ cup sugar
¼ cup sparkling white
   grape juice

EQUIPMENT

Measuring cups
Large mixing bowl
Wire whisk or eggbeater
Sharp knife
Cutting board
Fruit juicer
Small mixing bowl
Mixing spoon
6 glasses

*"Bub" is an English nickname
for a drink with bubbles!*

DIRECTIONS   *6 servings*

1. Measure the whipping cream into the large mixing bowl and beat it with the wire whisk or eggbeater until it is thick. Set the bowl aside.

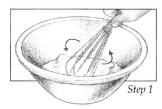

Step 1

2. Cut the lemons and orange in half.

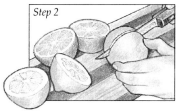

Step 2

3. Set the juicer over the small mixing bowl so the edges fit tightly.

4. Squeeze the juice out of the lemons and orange by turning them back and forth on the juicer while you push down.

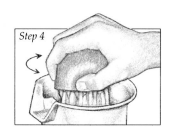

Step 4

5. Add the sugar and grape juice to the lemon and orange juice. Stir until blended.

6. Pour the juice mixture into the whipped cream. Stir just enough to blend the juices and cream. The syllabub should be thick and frothy. Serve it in individual glasses. 🥄

FAVORITE FOODS

A tea service.

Felicity practiced the tea ceremony at the home of Miss Manderly, her teacher. She loved to watch Miss Manderly gracefully scoop the dry tea leaves into the delicate china teapot. Along with the tea, Miss Manderly sometimes served two of Felicity's favorite sweets—tiny almond tarts and queen cakes filled with dark currants.

When the King of England placed a tax on tea, many colonial families, including the Merrimans, protested it. Colonists who did not agree with the king's rule were called *Patriots*. They refused to buy, sell, or drink tea. Instead, they made their own "liberty teas" from flowers, herbs, and fruit leaves. They also drank coffee and chocolate. In Felicity's time, chocolate was a drink, not a candy! A girl like Felicity would shave part of a roll or cake of solid chocolate into boiling water or milk. Then she served the drink from a chocolate pot.

A young girl adding sugar to her tea.

When Felicity visited Grandfather's plantation each summer, she was treated to delicious fruit desserts. Wild raspberries and blackberries grew near the woods, strawberries grew near the fields, and there were watermelons and muskmelons ripening in the melon patch.

In her own garden, Felicity grew herbs and vegetables near the kitchen and sweet-smelling flowers near the house, just as Grandfather had taught her. She was most pleased with her pumpkins, but they ripened so slowly! Even though Mother reminded Felicity that the pumpkins would not grow faster just to please her, Felicity was still impatient. Each morning she tried to guess which one would taste best in her favorite dessert—baked pumpkin pudding!

FAVORITE FOODS

Beefsteak Pie

•

Baked Pumpkin Pudding

•

Raspberry Flummery

•

Almond Tarts

•

Queen Cakes

•

Spiced Nuts

•

Liberty Tea

BEEFSTEAK PIE

Colonists ate beefsteak pie warm for dinner and cold for supper or breakfast!

INGREDIENTS

Two pastry piecrusts
   for 9-inch pie pan
1- to 2-pound beef
   rump roast
Salt and pepper
1 tablespoon cooking oil
2 tablespoons flour
4 tablespoons water
2 cups beef broth
1 teaspoon dried parsley
$\frac{1}{8}$ teaspoon marjoram
$\frac{1}{8}$ teaspoon savory
$\frac{1}{8}$ teaspoon thyme
2 tablespoons butter

EQUIPMENT

9-inch pie pan
Sharp knife
Cutting board
Rolling pin
Measuring cup
   and spoons
Large skillet
Fork
Small bowl
Wooden spoon
Butter knife
Potholders
Trivet
Pie server

DIRECTIONS   *6 servings*

Step 1

1. Line the bottom of the pie pan with 1 of the piecrusts.

2. Have an adult slice the rump roast into small, thin steaks about $\frac{1}{4}$ inch thick.

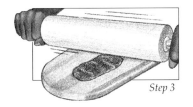

Step 3

3. Put the steaks on a cutting board or counter and pound them with the rolling pin until they are tender. Sprinkle the steaks with salt and pepper.

Step 4

4. Heat the cooking oil in the skillet over medium heat. Put the steaks into the skillet. Use the fork to turn over the steaks several times to brown them on both sides. Use the fork to move the steaks into the pastry-lined pie pan. Set the pan aside.

5. Preheat the oven to 400°. Measure the flour and water into the bowl and stir with the fork to make a smooth paste.

6. Measure the beef broth into the skillet and heat it until it *boils*, or bubbles quickly.

7. To make a gravy, stir the flour paste slowly into the broth with the wooden spoon. When the gravy is thick, turn down the heat. Let the gravy *simmer*, or bubble gently, for 3 minutes.

8. Sprinkle salt and pepper over the gravy and stir. Then have an adult help you pour the gravy over the steaks in the pie pan.

9. Sprinkle parsley, marjoram, savory, and thyme over the steaks and gravy.

10. Cut the butter into small pieces. Dot the top of the pie with butter.

11. Cover the pie with the other piecrust. Press the edges of the bottom and top crusts together to seal them. Cut six small slits in the top of the piecrust.

12. Bake the pie for 50 minutes, or until the crust is golden brown. Have an adult remove the pie from the oven. Place the pie on a trivet at the table and serve. 🥄

PRESERVING MEATS

Colonists often preserved fresh meat for winter by salting it. First the meat was salted on both sides. Then it was buried under salt in a trough like the one shown here for up to six weeks. After that, colonists either smoked the meat or put it into barrels of salty water, or **brine,** *where the meat soaked until they were ready to cook it.*

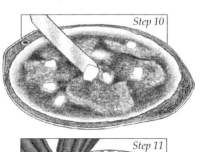

Step 10

Step 11

BAKED PUMPKIN PUDDING

Felicity used her best pumpkin to make this tasty pudding.

INGREDIENTS

4 eggs
1-pound can of pumpkin
1 teaspoon cinnamon
1/2 teaspoon ginger
1/4 teaspoon allspice
1/2 cup molasses
1 cup milk
Butter or shortening to
   grease casserole dish

EQUIPMENT

Large mixing bowl
Fork
Wooden spoon
Measuring cups
   and spoons
Paper towels
1 1/2-quart casserole dish
Potholders
Trivet
Serving spoon

DIRECTIONS   *6 servings*

1. Preheat the oven to 350°.

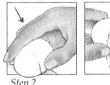

Step 2

2. Crack the eggs into the large mixing bowl. Beat them with the fork until they are light yellow. Add the canned pumpkin to the eggs and mix well with the wooden spoon.

3. Measure the cinnamon, ginger, and allspice into the mixing bowl. Add the molasses and milk. Stir well.

4. Use paper towels to grease the casserole dish with butter or shortening. Pour the pumpkin mixture into the casserole dish.

5. Bake the pudding for 1 hour. Then have an adult take the casserole dish out of the oven. Put the casserole dish on a trivet at the table and serve the pudding. 🌿

COOKING WITH PUMPKINS

Pumpkins were introduced to the colonists by American Indians. Pumpkins are easy to grow, and colonial cooks invented many new ways to prepare them. Since pumpkins dry and store well, they were used throughout the winter in puddings and other dishes.

RASPBERRY FLUMMERY

INGREDIENTS

3 cups raspberries
¾ cup cold water
1 cup sugar
½ teaspoon salt
6 tablespoons cornstarch

EQUIPMENT

Colander
Measuring cups
  and spoons
3-quart saucepan with lid
Wooden spoon
Small bowl
Fork
6 small glass dishes

DIRECTIONS   *6 servings*

1. Put the raspberries into the colander and rinse them under cold running water at the sink.

2. Measure the water into the saucepan. Add the berries. Turn the heat to medium high.

3. Cover the saucepan and cook the berries about 10 minutes, or until they are soft. Stir them once or twice while they cook.

4. While the berries are cooking, measure the sugar, salt, and cornstarch into the bowl and stir them with the fork.

5. Slowly add the sugar mixture to the cooked berries and stir. Turn the heat to low and cook the mixture for another 10 minutes, or until it becomes thick.

6. Spoon the flummery into glass dishes. Chill the dishes in the refrigerator before serving. 🌸

Flummery was often the featured dessert at the end of an elegant dinner.

FANCY FLUMMERY

Colonial cooks shaped flummery in jelly molds, and they tinted it, too. Spinach juice created a green tint, syrup of violets made blue, egg yolks made yellow, chocolate made brown, and cream made white. One cook molded flummery into fish shapes. She served the fish in a "pond" of clear jelly!

ALMOND TARTS

Felicity baked tarts in tiny pans made of tin, brass, or stoneware.

INGREDIENTS

Pastry:

¾ cup flour
6 tablespoons butter
1 egg
1 tablespoon cream
Extra flour for rolling
  out dough

Filling:

½ cup butter
1 lemon
1 cup ground almonds
1 tablespoon orange juice
3 eggs
½ cup sugar

EQUIPMENT

Measuring cups
  and spoons
Medium mixing bowl
Pastry cutter or fork
Wooden spoon
Small saucepan
Grater
Large mixing bowl
Cutting board
Rolling pin
Muffin pan
Butter knife
Potholders

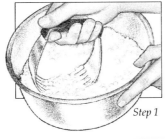

Step 1

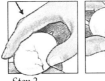

Step 2

DIRECTIONS   *12 tarts*

1. To make the pastry dough, measure the flour and butter into the medium mixing bowl. Use the pastry cutter or fork to blend them until the mixture is crumbly.

2. Crack the egg into the bowl. Add the cream and stir to form a smooth dough.

3. Chill the pastry dough for 15 to 30 minutes in the refrigerator.

4. While the dough is chilling, preheat the oven to 325°.

5. To make the filling, melt the butter in the saucepan over low heat.

6. Grate the outer, yellow part of the lemon peel. Measure 1 tablespoon of grated lemon peel into the large mixing bowl.

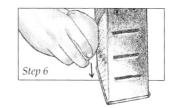

Step 6

7. Add the melted butter, ground almonds, orange juice, eggs, and sugar. Mix well. Set the bowl aside.

8. Remove the pastry dough from the refrigerator. Divide it into 12 pieces. Shape each piece into a ball.

9. On a floured cutting board, roll out each ball into a thin circle, about ¼ inch thick.

10. Fit each circle into a cup in the muffin pan. Pat the sides to make them fit like tiny pie crusts.

11. Put 2 tablespoons of filling into each muffin cup. Divide any remaining filling evenly among the cups.

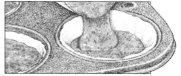

Steps 9, 10, 11

12. Bake the almond tarts for 40 minutes, or until a knife inserted in the center comes out clean.

13. Have an adult remove the tarts from the oven. Let them cool before serving. 🌿

QUEEN CAKES

Rich queen cakes were a colonial favorite all year round.

INGREDIENTS

Shortening or butter to
  grease pan
Flour to coat greased pan
$1/2$ cup butter, softened
$1/2$ cup sugar
2 eggs
2 tablespoons rose water*
$1/4$ teaspoon mace
$1/4$ teaspoon salt
1 cup flour
1 tablespoon flour
$1/4$ cup currants

Available at health-food and import stores and at some supermarkets.

EQUIPMENT

Paper towels
Muffin pan
Measuring cups
  and spoons
Medium mixing bowl
Wooden spoon
Small bowl
Potholders
Butter knife
Serving plate

DIRECTIONS   *12 cakes*

Step 1

1. Preheat the oven to 325°. Use paper towels to grease the muffin pan with shortening or butter. Then sprinkle flour over each muffin cup. Tap the pan so the flour coats each cup completely.

2. Put the softened butter into the mixing bowl. Add the sugar.

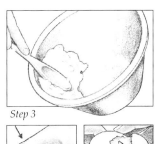
Step 3

3. Press the butter and sugar together against the side of the bowl until they are mixed. Then beat them together until they are creamy.

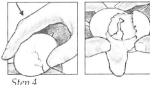
Step 4

4. Crack the eggs into the mixing bowl 1 at a time. Beat the mixture after adding each egg.

5. Add the rose water, mace, and salt. Beat well.

ROSE WATER

Rose water was a popular flavoring in Felicity's day. It was made by boiling rose petals in water.

6. Add 1 cup of flour to the mixture, ¼ cup at a time. Each time you add flour, beat the mixture until you have a smooth batter.

7. Put 1 tablespoon of flour into the small bowl. Add the currants and stir to coat them with flour. Then stir the currants into the batter.

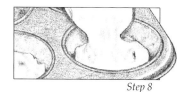

Step 8

8. Spoon 1 tablespoon of batter into each muffin cup. Divide any remaining batter evenly among the cups.

9. Bake the queen cakes for 40 minutes, or until they are golden brown.

Step 10

10. Have an adult remove the queen cakes from the oven. Use a butter knife to loosen the cakes from the muffin cups and move them to a serving plate. ❧

SUGAR CONES

In 1774, white sugar was pressed into a cone shape and packaged in blue paper. Colonial cooks pinched chunks of sugar from the cone with sugar nips, which look like tongs. No one knows why the wrapper was always blue, but colonists often soaked the color out of the paper and used it to dye fabric.

SPICED NUTS

Sugary, spicy nuts were the perfect ending to any colonial meal.

INGREDIENTS

Shortening or butter to
   grease cookie sheets
1 cup sugar
4 tablespoons cinnamon
¼ teaspoon nutmeg
2 eggs
1 cup pecans
1 cup almonds

EQUIPMENT

2 cookie sheets
Measuring cup
   and spoons
2 small bowls
Spoon
Fork
Potholders
Nut or candy dish

DIRECTIONS   *6 servings*

1. Preheat the oven to 300°. Grease the cookie sheets with shortening or butter.

2. Measure the sugar, cinnamon, and nutmeg into 1 of the small bowls and mix them.

Step 3

3. Have an adult help you separate the egg whites into the other small bowl as shown. Beat them with the fork. Then stir a few nuts into the egg whites.

4. Take the nuts out of the egg whites and roll them in the sugar and spice mixture.

5. Place the nuts on the cookie sheet. Prepare the rest of the nuts in the same way.

6. Bake the spiced nuts for 20 minutes. Have an adult remove the cookie sheets from the oven. Let the nuts cool, and then serve them in a pretty nut or candy dish. 🌿

LIBERTY TEA

INGREDIENTS

6 cups water
3 teaspoons dried
    raspberry leaves*
Honey
Available at health-food stores.

EQUIPMENT

Teakettle or saucepan
Measuring cup
    and spoons
Tea ball *(optional)*
Teapot
Strainer *(if you don't
    use a tea ball)*
6 teacups

*Felicity made tea from raspberry leaves
to protest the high tax on tea that
came from England.*

DIRECTIONS   *6 servings*

1. Pour the water into a teakettle or saucepan.
   Heat the water on high heat until it *boils*, or
   bubbles quickly.

2. Measure the raspberry leaves into the tea ball
   and place it in the teapot. Or measure the
   raspberry leaves directly into the teapot. Have
   an adult pour the boiling water into the teapot.
   Let the tea steep for 5 minutes.

Step 2

3. Remove the tea ball from the teapot and pour
   the tea into teacups. Or use the strainer to
   catch the tea leaves as you pour the tea into
   teacups. Sweeten the tea with honey.

Step 3

TEA BOWLS

*Families like the Merrimans had teatime
each day, between dinner in the early
afternoon and supper later in the evening.
They drank their tea from cups that had
no handles, often called **tea bowls**.*

41

PLAN A COLONIAL PARTY

INVITATIONS

Make invitations like the one Felicity received for the dancing lesson at the Governor's Palace. Use plain white notepaper and write an invitation with your prettiest handwriting. Fold the notepaper in thirds. Close the invitation with red sealing wax or tie a red ribbon around it. Deliver the invitations by hand or put them in envelopes for mailing.

Well-to-do Virginia colonists loved to get together for elegant teas, balls, and other entertainments. They celebrated weddings, special occasions, holidays, and—before the Revolutionary War—the birthdays of the King and Queen of England. During the Revolutionary War, some colonists had parties to celebrate victories over the British army. You can plan an elegant party just like one Felicity might have attended.

An Elegant Tea Party

Teatime was a tradition that colonial Americans brought with them from England. Every afternoon, friends and families gathered to share news and tell stories. It was a peaceful, relaxing part of the day.

Teatime was also a chance to practice proper manners. In Felicity's time, it was important to behave perfectly at the tea table, both as a hostess and as a guest. Guests discussed questions of general interest, so no one would be left out of the conversation.

Young gentlewomen like Felicity were expected to conduct the tea ceremony with grace and hospitality. When you serve tea, hand each guest a cup, saucer, and spoon. Have an adult help you pour tea for each guest. Offer your guests milk, sugar, or honey to put in their tea. Then offer tea biscuits or small cakes. Remember, a good hostess continues to fill each guest's teacup until the guest says that she will take no more tea. The polite way for a guest to refuse tea is to turn her teacup upside down and lay the teaspoon across it. Then she says, "Thank you. I shall take no tea."

❧ A Twelfth Night Party

In Felicity's time, the holiday season began in mid-December and lasted until January 6. To celebrate, people visited friends and family, attended balls and concerts, shared lavish meals, and sang carols. Colonists in Virginia celebrated the end of the holiday season on Twelfth Night, January 6. Twelfth Night is a celebration based on a Bible story. The story tells about the arrival of the Three Wise Men in Bethlehem, 12 days after Christmas. In colonial times, Twelfth Night was usually celebrated with lots of good food and sometimes a ball.

You can have a Twelfth Night party, too. Make some of the treats from this cookbook, such as raspberry flummery *(page 35)* and spiced nuts *(page 40)*. Then ask your parents if you can push aside the furniture in the largest room for dancing, just as Felicity's family might have.

Colonists in Virginia loved to dance. The minuet and country dances like jigs or reels were especially popular dances in colonial Virginia, but you and your guests can dance any way you like. If you can find someone who can play the fiddle or another instrument, you can dance to that music. Colonists would have danced by the light of candles, so you may want to light your room with a few candles, too. Sometimes extra mirrors, or *looking glasses* as they were called in Felicity's day, were hung on the walls to reflect the candlelight.

PLAYING GAMES

Games often followed a festive meal. People liked to play charades and blindman's buff, games that people still play today. Hide the Thimble was also popular. To play, all the guests leave the room except for one person, who hides a thimble somewhere in the room. The group then returns to look for it. The person who finds the thimble wins!

FLOWER DECORATIONS

You might like to decorate foods with the petals of flowers such as violets or roses, just as some colonists did. Use petals that have never been sprayed with insecticide. Sprinkle fresh petals on salads, or use candied petals to decorate desserts. To make candied petals, dip the petals in egg whites and then in sugar. Let them dry on a plate overnight.

Food

For a tea party, make some of the recipes from this cookbook, such as almond tarts *(page 36)*, queen cakes *(page 38)*, or liberty tea *(page 41)*. If you have a Twelfth Night party, make a white cake and hide a bean inside it. Then cover the cake with white icing. When you serve slices to your guests, tell them to look for the bean. The person who gets the bean is named queen or king of the party!

Place Settings

Cover your table with a white tablecloth. Put a white cloth napkin by each place setting. Ask to use your family's best dishes. Or use plastic dishes that look as though they are made of silver or fine china. They are available in some party shops.

Decorations

It was popular among wealthy Virginia colonists to put a few small ceramic figurines of people or animals on the dining table. For a centerpiece, a pyramid made of fruits such as apples, pears, lemons, and pineapples was fashionable.

Clothes

Tell your guests to wear long dresses or skirts if they can. Colonial girls and women liked to use fans, so you might want to make or purchase inexpensive fans to give to your guests as favors.

Music

You can find recordings of classical music from the 1700s, such as the music by Johann Sebastian Bach, at the library. You and your guests can also sing "Yankee Doodle Dandy," which was popular during the American Revolution!

AMERICAN GIRLS PASTIMES®
Activities from the Past for Girls of Today

You'll enjoy all the Pastimes books about your favorite characters in The American Girls Collection®.

Learn to cook foods that Felicity, Josefina, Kirsten, Addy, Samantha, and Molly loved. The Pastimes **COOKBOOKS** are filled with great recipes and fun party ideas.

Make the same crafts that your favorite American Girls characters made. Each of the **CRAFT BOOKS** has simple step-by-step instructions and fascinating historical facts.

Imagine that you are your favorite American Girls character as you stage a play about her. Each of the **THEATER KITS** has four Play Scripts and a Director's Guide.

Learn about fashions of the past as you cut out the ten outfits in each of the **PAPER DOLL KITS.** Each kit also contains a make-it-yourself book plus historical fun facts.

There is also a **CRAFT BOOK & KIT** for each character with supplies to make three crafts from the Craft Book.

Pastimes books and kits are available at fine bookstores everywhere.

Turn the page to learn more about the other delights in The American Girls Collection. ⟶

I'm an American girl who loves to get mail. Please send me a catalogue of The American Girls Collection®:

My name is _____

My address is _____

City _____ State _____ Zip _____

Parent's signature _____

1961

And send a catalogue to my friend:

My friend's name is _____

Address _____

City _____ State _____ Zip _____

1225

Detach card at perforated lines.

THE AMERICAN GIRLS COLLECTION®

The American Girls Collection tells the stories of six lively girls who lived long ago—Felicity, Josefina, Kirsten, Addy, Samantha, and Molly. You can read about their adventures in a series of beautifully illustrated books of historical fiction. You'll learn what growing up was like in times past.

And while books are the heart of The American Girls Collection, they are only the beginning. Our lovable dolls and their beautiful clothes and accessories make the stories in The American Girls Collection come alive.

The American Girls Collection is for you if you love to curl up with a good book. It's for you if you like to play with dolls and act out stories. It's for you if you want to collect something so special that you will treasure it for years to come.

To learn more about The American Girls Collection, fill out the postcard on the other side of the page and mail it to Pleasant Company, or call **1-800-845-0005**. We'll send you a free catalogue full of books, dolls, dresses, and other delights for girls.

BUSINESS REPLY MAIL
FIRST-CLASS MAIL   PERMIT NO. 1137   MIDDLETON WI

POSTAGE WILL BE PAID BY ADDRESSEE

PLEASANT COMPANY®

PO BOX 620497
MIDDLETON WI 53562-9940

NO POSTAGE
NECESSARY
IF MAILED
IN THE
UNITED STATES